# CONTENTS

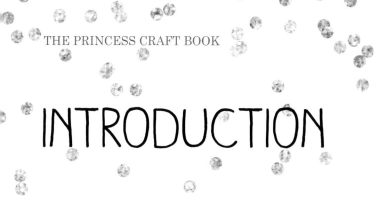

# INTRODUCTION

Every princess needs a suitable collection of clothes, accessories, toys, and games to stay entertained and properly attired. That is what this book is for—to provide everything needed for one's royal activities. These pages are filled with exciting projects for you and your little princess to make together. You will find everything you need to create a full princess kit—from tutus and tiaras to puppets and ponies. We even show you how to throw a princess party.

The 15 projects vary in terms of length and time required, but all are suitable for beginners and busy parents. Each project is broken down into illustrated step-by-step instructions to make it as clear as possible. Templates, when needed, can be found at the back of the book (see page 62).

Many of the projects can be made by a child, with a little assistance and supervision from an adult. The remainder are designed to be made by an adult, but many have fun elements that a child can get involved with as well.

We appreciate that not all girls are into pink, princessy things, and that many boys, in fact, are. We applaud those children who don't conform to stereotypes, but we can't deny that many kids are obsessed with all things to do with princesses, and that is why we have created this book.

We are busy parents to four kids, and our own little girls love dressing up and pretending to be princesses. We love making things for, and with, our children and we're very lucky to spend a lot of our time crafting. We established our blog, *Little Button Diaries*, as a way of documenting the things we make for our little ones. We wanted to show other parents that you don't need a lot of time or craft skills to make fun stuff. As our blog has grown, so have our children, and we find ourselves making more things to reflect the princess mania that has swept over our households. The 15 projects in this book have all had our "Little Buttons" royal seal of approval—tried and tested by our very own little princesses.

# TOOLS AND MATERIALS

We have tried to ensure that all of the materials featured in this book are those that people will have at home, or be able to buy easily. You will require some basic supplies for some of the projects and these are outlined below.

## Art and craft supplies

We recommend building up a good stock of art supplies in order to be craft-ready at all times. Arm yourself with the following and you and your kids will be able to whip up a crown or wand at a moment's notice.

PVA glue, glue stick, and strong glue
Pipe cleaners
Stick-on gems
Glitter and glitter glue
Colored card
Foam sheets
Cardboard boxes and tubes
Pompoms
Scissors

### Paint and brushes

We used acrylic paint for these projects as it gives a thicker and more resistant finish, but ready-mixed poster paint is a good child-friendly alternative. For an even coverage, apply several coats. A variety of different-sized brushes would be useful to have to hand.

### Polymer clay

This is a malleable, colored clay that is baked in the oven. It's great for children because it's brightly colored and really easy to use. We prefer to use the soft type as it's much easier to work. It is available in craft stores and online in a large variety of colors.

### Salt dough

This can easily be made from kitchen-cupboard staples. It's similar to modeling dough, but you bake it in the oven to harden. It can then be painted (but not eaten!). For the recipe, see the Salt-Dough Twinkle Wand project on page 16.

## Sewing supplies

You will need a selection of colored sewing threads as well as some embroidery thread—a thicker yarn than that used on a machine—for the hand stitching. Pins, needles, and fabric scissors are essential.

### Sewing machine

Five of the projects in this book involve sewing. A sewing machine will really help you, particularly to stitch up the winter cape, handbag, horse, and skirt. These could all be sewn by hand, but they would take a lot longer. We have assumed a basic knowledge of how to use a sewing machine in the instructions.

### Fabrics

Those used in this book include polar fleece, corduroy, organza, and felt. Where possible, alternatives are suggested. Felt is a particularly good material to have on hand because it doesn't fray, it's cheap, and it can be glued or stitched.

### Ribbons, yarn, trims, bells, and buttons

These all crop up in the book at some point. They are readily available in all craft stores. Where necessary, we have stated the width of ribbon within the projects.

When purchasing thread or ribbon, it's always handy to have a small piece of your fabric with you so that you can easily match the colors.

# HEART HANDBAG AND CHARM

Kids love bags. In them, they can pack away their most precious treasures and take them out for the day. This heart handbag is easy to make and a great introduction to sewing for beginners. We made this one from red corduroy, but it can be made from any fabric as long as it is relatively thick. Both the bag and charms can be made in other shapes as well—as long as they are not too complex.

## You will need

- ♡ 20in (50cm) red corduroy fabric
- ♡ 20in (50cm) coordinating fabric for the lining
- ♡ 1yd (1m) length of string
- ♡ Scraps of faux gold and silver leather
- ♡ Masking tape
- ♡ Metal key ring
- ♡ 2 x metal snap fasteners

- ♡ Hammer
- ♡ Scissors
- ♡ Sewing machine
- ♡ Heart, lock, and key templates found on page 62

4

## Step 1

Photocopy the heart template found on page 62 and cut it out. Use the template to cut out two hearts from the corduroy fabric, and two from the lining fabric. Transfer the position marks for the bag opening onto the corduroy pieces.

## Step 2

Pin the two corduroy pieces together with right sides facing, leaving a 5in (12.5cm) opening along the top. With a ½in (1cm) seam allowance, sew around the edge of the heart where the pins are, leaving the top section open. Repeat for the two lining fabric pieces. Cut notches in the fabric, all the way around on both hearts, then turn the corduroy heart the right way out. Fold the notches along the top inward and press all over with an iron. Keep the lining fabric heart inside out, fold the notches outward and press.

## Step 3

To make the strap, cut a strip of corduroy 37in (95cm) long by 2in (5cm) wide. Take the string, and place it along the center of the right side of the strip of fabric (this will help you to turn the strap the right way out in the next step.) Fold the strip of fabric in half lengthways over the string and pin in place with right sides together. Stitch across one end of the string to secure it down. Sew along the long edge of the fabric with a ½in (1cm) seam allowance.

## Step 4

To turn the strap the right way out, take the end of the fabric not sewn to the string and fold it back on itself. Holding the string in one hand, gradually pull the fabric the right way out. This can be a little fiddly to start with, but it gets easier the further along you get. Cut off the string and iron the strap flat.

## Step 5

Put your hand inside the lining fabric heart and insert it into the bag. Pin all the way around the top, making sure the notches are all facing inward and are sandwiched between the layers. Take a couple of pins and insert the ends of the strap at each side of the heart where the markers are, in between the corduroy and the lining. Leave 1in (2.5cm) of extra strap at each end and pin in place. Stitch the bag and lining together by hand.

## Step 6

Mark out with a dot of ink where to place the snap fasteners on the front of the bag. To attach them, follow the manufacturer's instructions—they will need to be attached either with thread or hammered in place. For the back, clip the loose fastener onto the front piece and mark in pen where it should be positioned.

## Step 7

To make the key-ring charm, photocopy the lock and key templates from page 62 and cut them out. Cut out two squares of leather a little bigger than the template for each charm. Place the two pieces of leather wrong sides together and tape together, using masking tape, to stop them from slipping. Trace around the templates with pencil.

## Step 8

Sew around the edge of each template, including the inner part of the lock and the holes for attaching them to the key ring. Remove the template and masking tape and trim away the excess leather close to the stitch line. Carefully cut away the inner part of the lock and the holes. The charms can then be attached to a key ring and clipped onto the side of the bag.

If you are using hammered snap fasteners rather than stitch-on ones, have a trial

run on scrap fabric first. Once they are attached to the bag, they are tricky to remove!

# SHRINK-PLASTIC JEWELS

Diamonds are a girl's best friend... but why stop there? With these shrink-plastic jewels, you can have rubies, sapphires, or emeralds to liven up any princess outfit. Shrink plastic is a fun craft material for children to use because it is as easy as drawing a picture! This tutorial is for a simple ribbon necklace, but you could create other accessories such as hair clips, badges, or key rings.

## You will need

- ♡ 5 x sheets of white shrink plastic measuring 4 x 6in (10 x 15cm)
- ♡ Pencil and eraser
- ♡ Permanent fine-line markers in various colors
- ♡ Crayons in various colors
- ♡ Hole punch
- ♡ 30in (75cm) of fine ⅛in (3mm) wide ribbon, or a necklace
- ♡ Tracing paper
- ♡ Scissors
- ♡ Baking sheet
- ♡ Jewel templates found on page 62

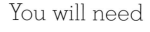

## USING SHRINK PLASTIC

Bear in mind a few things when making things from shrink plastic. Firstly, it shrinks! Work out the size you want your finished piece to be, then enlarge this by about six times, or you may end up with something bigger or smaller than you wanted. Secondly, the colors will intensify when they shrink, so try to color the plastic slightly paler than you would like. Finally, use markers or pencils that are not water soluble or you will end up with ink on your fingers!

## Step 1

Begin by drawing the jewels in pencil onto the rough side of the shrink plastic. If you like, you can photocopy or trace the templates found on page 62, or create your own designs. Once you are happy with them, go over the pencil lines in permanent marker and rub out the pencil with an eraser.

## Step 2

Color in the jewels with crayons and then cut them out. Make sure to snip off the very ends of any sharp edges, as these would become quite sharp once shrunk.

## Step 3

With a hole punch, make two holes on each jewel, near the top outer edge on each side. These enable the jewels to be threaded onto a ribbon.

## Step 4

Preheat the oven to 325°F/160°C/Gas Mark 3. Place the jewels on a baking sheet and space them well apart.

## Step 5

Put the baking sheet in the oven, then watch the magic happen! The jewels will only take a few minutes to shrink down. The plastic will curl about at first, but after a couple of minutes it will settle flat. Don't remove it from the oven until the plastic has flattened completely.

## Step 6

Knot each end of the ribbon so it doesn't unravel. Then thread the jewels onto the ribbon to make a necklace fit for a princess.

If you want your jewels to shine, the plastic can be covered with craft varnish.

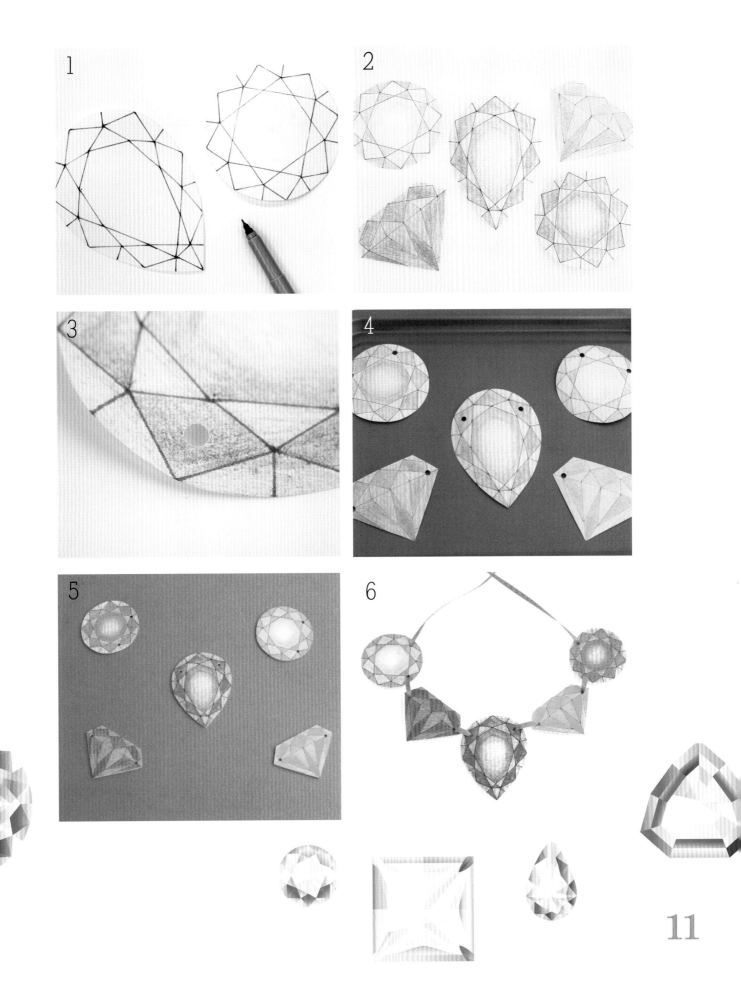

# SECRET CASTLE TRINKET BOX

Every princess needs somewhere to store precious things, and this one is extra special because it has hidden compartments to deter unwanted intruders. The top tier lifts up to store larger items, while the drawbridge opens to reveal a secret space for hiding precious jewels (shhh!). Little ones can get their royal hands messy by using papier-mâché and paint. Pop a mini polymer-clay princess into one of the turrets to watch over all of your favorite keepsakes.

## You will need

- An adult-sized shoebox with lid
- A medium-sized square cardboard box with lid, roughly 8 x 8in (20 x 20cm)
- A small square box without a lid, roughly 4 x 4in (10 x 10cm)
- Newspaper
- PVA glue
- Strong glue
- Masking tape
- Blue, pink, and silver acrylic paint
- Pink and yellow embroidery thread
- 4 x cardboard tubes, roughly 5in (12.5cm) long
- 1 x small cardboard tube, roughly 2½in (6.5cm) long
- Small amount of polymer clay in pale pink and purple (about a ½in/1cm cube of each)
- Black permanent fine-line marker
- 1 x piece of plain card, 8 x 12in (20 x 30cm)
- 1 x piece of corrugated card, 8 x 12in (20 x 30cm)
- Scraps of colored card
- Hook-and-loop tape
- Scissors
- Craft knife
- Sewing needle
- Paintbrush or glue spreader

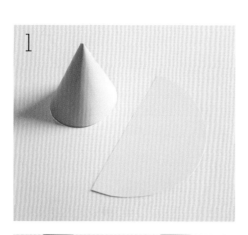

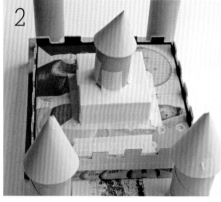

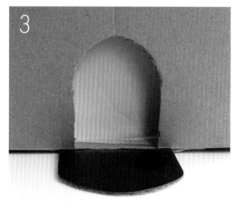

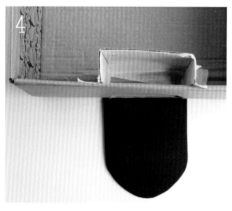

## Step 1

Begin by making the turrets. Cut three circles from plain card, roughly 4in (10cm) in diameter. Cut these in half, then fold five of the half-circles and tape each one together to create cones a little wider than the ends of the cardboard tubes. Using strong glue, attach the cones onto the top of the five tubes.

## Step 2

To assemble the top of the castle, use strong glue to connect the smaller box onto the lid of the bigger box. Turn the smallest box so that the open side is underneath and tape it onto the lid of the medium box. Attach the turrets with masking tape; one on each corner of the lid of the bigger box and the smallest one in the middle of the small box. Cut a strip of square battlements (as shown) from card and, using strong glue, attach these along the lid of the medium box.

## Step 3

To make the drawbridge, draw a door shape onto the front of the bigger box and cut it out. From the piece of corrugated card, cut a door shape that is 1in (2.5cm) bigger than the first door you drew, with an additional 1in (2.5cm) tab at the bottom to allow it to be fixed on. To attach the drawbridge, tape the tab onto the bottom of the box, under the opening on the front of the box.

## Step 4

For the secret compartment behind the drawbridge, cut a rectangle out of cardboard that is the same height as the bigger box and 2in (5cm) wider than the door. Fold over 1in (2.5cm) on each side to form two walls. Position the compartment behind the drawbridge and tape it in place. Add a top to the compartment by cutting out a piece of cardboard to fit, and use some masking tape to secure it in place.

## Step 5

Cover surfaces and put on aprons before you begin—this part can be messy! To make papier-mâché, tear up squares of newspaper and mix a paste of two parts PVA glue to one part water. Separate the different parts of the castle, then dip newspaper into the paste and place it down flat, covering the entire thing. Leave the papier-mâché to completely dry out overnight and repeat the process until you have three layers of newspaper.

## Step 6

Paint the inside of the box and the drawbridge silver, then paint the outside blue with pink turret tops. Finally, add a heart motif on the drawbridge in blue paint.

## Step 7

Once the paint is dry, cut a small window from one of the turrets with a craft knife, about 1in (2.5cm) high. Paint black windows onto the other turrets.

Why not add personalized flags, banners, or bunting made from card and string?

## Step 8

Glue a small piece of hook-and-loop tape to the top of the drawbridge and the wall to enable it to close. Thread a short length of pink embroidery thread onto a sewing needle, knot the end, then puncture through the drawbridge and the castle wall to make the chains. Knot again at the end to secure.

## Step 9

To create your little Rapunzel, roll ½in (1cm) of purple polymer clay into a sausage with a slightly wider base to make the body. For the head, roll a pea-sized piece of pale pink polymer clay and press it onto the top of the body. For the arms, roll a thin piece of purple polymer clay to about 1in (2.5cm) long and attach two peppercorn-sized balls of pink clay to the ends. Cut in half and press in place on the body. Pinch the body at the bottom so that it is flatter, in order to glue it inside the window. Bake in the oven, following the manufacturer's guidelines.

## Step 10

To make Rapunzel's golden locks, take some yellow embroidery thread and wrap it six times around a small book (about 8in/20cm). Gently ease the wrapped thread off the book then, holding the center of the thread, glue onto the top and back of the head. Once dry, trim the ends off and plait the hair. Secure the plait by tying embroidery thread around it. Rapunzel is then ready to be positioned inside her window using strong glue.

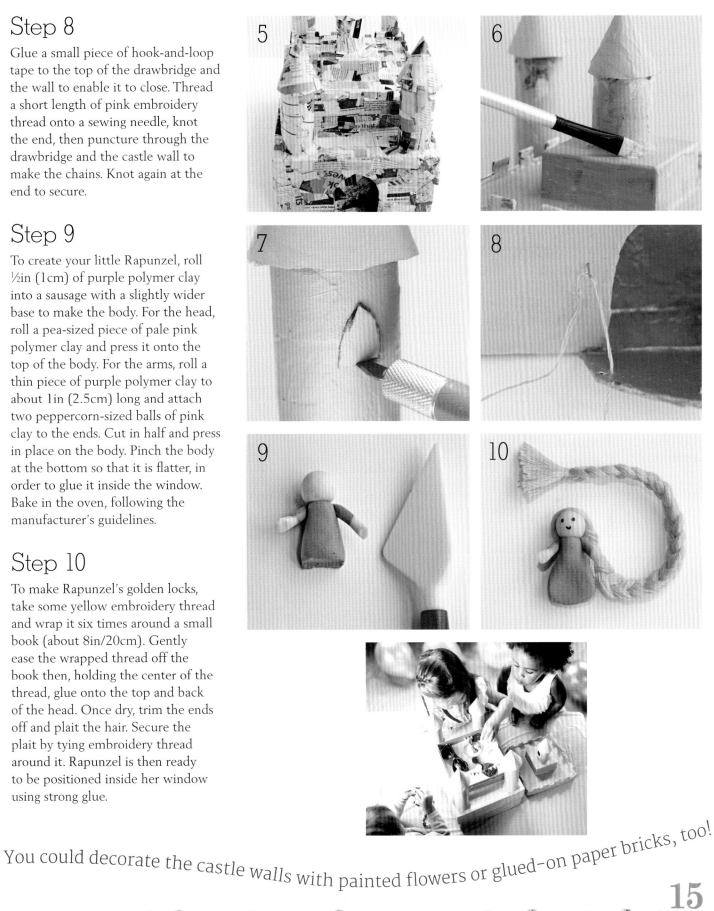

You could decorate the castle walls with painted flowers or glued-on paper bricks, too!

# SALT-DOUGH TWINKLE WAND

It's magical being a princess, especially when holding your own wonderful wand. This project uses salt dough, which is very simple to make as it uses only three basic ingredients. You could make a set of wands using cookie cutters to create different shapes—decorating them would make a great princess party activity (see page 56 for other fun party ideas).

## You will need

### For the salt dough:

- 8oz (225g) flour
- 8oz (225g) salt
- 4fl oz (100ml) lukewarm water

### For the wand:

- Pink acrylic paint
- 10in (25cm) length of doweling, ¼in (6mm) thick
- A roll of pretty fabric washi tape, ½in (1cm) wide

- ½in (1cm) glue-on gems
- Strong glue
- 3 x pieces of different-colored narrow ribbon, 8in (20cm) long
- 3 x small bells
- Sewing needle and thread
- Rolling pin
- Star-shaped cookie cutter, about 2½in (6cm) wide
- Plastic wrap

# Step 1

Begin by making the salt dough. Preheat the oven to 210°F/100°C/ Gas Mark ¼. Mix the flour and salt together. Add the water in small amounts, and mix together to form a dough. The dough should not be sticky or come off on your fingers. If it does, add more flour to the mix. Knead into a ball then roll out to a thickness of ½in (1cm).

# Step 2

Use a cookie cutter or paper template to cut out a star shape about 2½in (6cm) wide. Poke the dowel into the bottom edge of the star to make a hole in the dough.

# Step 3

Bake the star in the oven for 2–3 hours, until the dough has hardened and turned slightly brown, turning over halfway through. Remove from the oven and leave to cool.

# Step 4

Once the star has cooled down, paint it all over with two coats of pink acrylic paint. Once it is dry, use strong glue to attach the gems around the edge.

# Step 5

Wrap the fabric washi tape diagonally around the dowel in order to cover it completely. Secure at each end with a dab of glue.

Placing plastic wrap on your work surface before rolling the dough makes it easier

6

7

## Step 6

Check the dowel fits inside the hole in the star—it may have lost its shape a little with cooking, in which case you may need to twist the handle of a teaspoon into the hole to widen it. Put some strong glue into the hole and press the ends of each of the lengths of narrow ribbon inside. Add a little more glue, then insert the dowel, pushing it into the hole as far as it will go.

## Step 7

Finally, hand stitch the small bells onto the ends of each of the ribbons.

to remove when cut into shape.

# WINTER PRINCESS CAPE

This warm and cuddly fleece cape is the perfect addition to an ice princess costume. Polar fleece is a great fabric for beginner sewers because it doesn't fray, so the edges can be left raw. The fleece could be swapped for a lighter fabric for a cooler look—the pattern is very simple and will remain the same. If you use a lighter fabric, you will need to sew the edges under or use bias binding. You can also get creative with the embellishments—this cape features pompoms and feathers, but you could try jewels, fabric paint, or even monogram the back in felt.

## You will need

♡ 2yd (1.8m) purple polar fleece

♡ 1yd (1m) length of 1in (2.5cm) wide pink ribbon

♡ 1½yd (1.25m) length of pompom trim

♡ 1yd (1m) length of light purple feather-boa trim

♡ Tailor's chalk

♡ Ruler

♡ Safety pin

♡ Sewing needle and matching thread

♡ Pins

♡ Sewing machine

# PATTERN GUIDELINES

## Outer cape piece

Top

9¼in (23cm)

17¾in (45cm)

Fold

15¾in (40cm)

## Inner cape piece

Top

6¼in (16cm)

Fold

33½in (85cm)

15¾in (40cm)

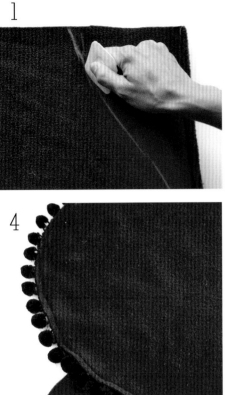

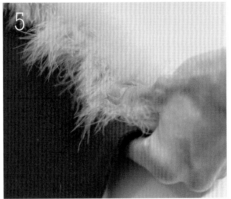

## Step 1

First, fold the fabric in half and mark out the shape of the cape as shown in the diagram opposite, using a ruler and tailor's chalk. Use the drawing as a guide—the dimensions do not have to be exact because the garment is not fitted. You may find it easier to draw around a circular dinner plate to get a smooth curve for the outer cape.

## Step 2

Lay the outer cape piece out flat. Then place the inner piece on top, 2in (5cm) from the top edge of the outer fabric, positioned in the center. There should be about 2in (5cm) of outer cape fabric on each side of the inner piece.

## Step 3

Fold the 2in (5cm) of outer cape over the inner cape and pin together, sandwiching the fabric in place. Sew along the edge of the fabric to create a channel for the ribbon.

## Step 4

Pin the length of pompom trim around the lower edge of the outer cape and sew it in place.

## Step 5

Take the length of feather-boa trim and line it up around the bottom edge of the inner cape piece. Hand stitch it in place, all the way along.

## Step 6

Take the ribbon and fold each end over by ½in (1cm) and secure with a few hand stitches. Attach a safety pin onto one end of the ribbon and gradually feed it through the channel at the top of the cape, wiggling and pulling it along. Hold onto one end so that it does not get lost as you pull the other end through. Tie the ribbon in a bow to hold the cape in place when being worn.

# THREE QUICK CROWNS

These three crowns are fantastic for all royal occasions. The mini glitter crown is attached to a hair clip, so it can be fastened onto the hair in any position, perfect for an understated royal look. The sparkly pipe-cleaner crown is so easy to make, using just two materials. Pipe cleaners are fantastic for crafting—they're cheap, versatile, and easy to work with. The felt tiara is stylish and simple. Because it stays in place with a plastic hairband, even the youngest princess can wear it without fear of it falling off. The shape can be as elaborate as you like, but remember that you will need to cut it from felt, so avoid drawing anything too fiddly.

## You will need

### For the mini crown hair clip:

- 6 x 8in (15 x 20cm) silver glitter foam
- Strong glue
- Hair clip
- Small white pompoms
- Pink acrylic paint
- Paint brush
- Safety pin
- Template for the mini crown found on page 63

### For the pipe-cleaner crown:

- Approximately 14 gold or silver sparkly pipe cleaners
- Approximately 22 mixed beads, big enough to fit onto the pipe cleaners

### For the felt tiara:

- 1 x plain plastic hair band
- 8 x 12in (20 x 30cm) white sparkly felt
- PVA glue
- Sewing needle and thread
- Scissors

# MINI CROWN HAIR CLIP

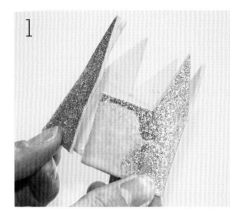

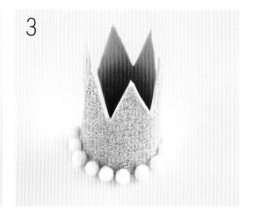

## Step 1

Photocopy the crown template found on page 63. Draw around it onto the glitter foam and cut it out with scissors. Roll it into a tube shape with the tab on the inside, and glue it in place. Press together and hold until the glue has set enough to stay in place.

## Step 2

To make the base, place the crown on top of another sheet of glitter foam and draw around the inside. Cut this out and glue it inside the bottom of the crown.

## Step 3

Glue the pompoms along the bottom outer edge of the crown and paint the inside pink. Finally, glue the hair clip onto the base and leave to dry completely—you don't want glue in your hair!

# PIPE-CLEANER CROWN

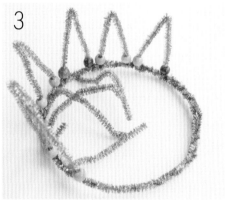

## Step 1

Begin by making a hoop shape from two pipe cleaners, a little smaller than the circumference of your child's head (roughly 5in/12.5cm in diameter). Twist the ends together.

## Step 2

Take another pipe cleaner and fold it in half to make an upside down 'V' shape. Place a bead onto each end and slide until each one is about 3in (8cm) from the bend at the top. Twist each side of the 'V' shape to secure it onto the hoop, to form the spikes of the crown.

## Step 3

Repeat this process around the entire loop. Take the excess pipe cleaner ends and twist them around the hoop of the crown.

# FELT TIARA

1

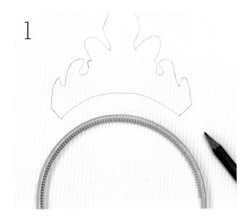

2

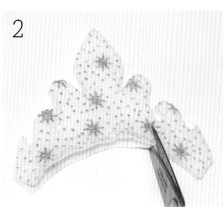

3

## Step 1

Begin by making a template for the felt. Place the hair band on a piece of paper and draw around the top curve. Draw your design for the tiara on top of this curve (fold the paper in half along the curve if you want it to be symmetrical). Add an additional ½in (1cm) below the curve to enable it to be attached to the hair band. Cut the shape out.

## Step 2

Pin the template to the piece of felt and cut out two pieces—a front and a back piece (remember to turn the template over if it is not symmetrical). Glue the two pieces together, leaving the bottom ½in (1cm) tab unglued. Once dry, make snips all the way along the bottom, ½in (1cm) apart.

## Step 3

Once dried, place the hair band inside these tabs. Add a little glue to the middle to stop it from sliding off the band, then fold in the tabs and hand stitch together with a needle and thread.

# ICE PRINCESS TUTU

This skirt is simply too, too elegant! Made from lightweight organza, the skirt wraps around the waist and ties with ribbon, so sizing isn't overly important. Organza is a lovely delicate fabric that comes in different weights—the finer it is, the more fiddly it will be to sew. You could also use tulle (netting) if you want a puffier, ballerina look. Go for any color combination you like, adding more layers for extra puff! This project isn't as tricky as it looks, so don't be put off if you're new to sewing.

## You will need

- 2yd (1.8m) length of pale blue organza or fine tulle
- 2yd (1.8m) length of white organza or fine tulle
- 4¼yd (4m) length of ½in (1cm) wide blue ribbon
- 2yd (1.8m) length of ½in (1cm) wide white ribbon
- 2yd (1.8m) length of 4in (10cm) wide blue ribbon
- Approximately ten snowflake embellishments
- Strong glue
- Sewing machine
- Matching thread
- Iron
- Scissors

## SIZE CHART

| Age (years) | Approximate waist measurement |
| --- | --- |
| 3 | 20½in (52cm) |
| 4 | 21in (53cm) |
| 5 | 21½in (55cm) |
| 6 | 22in (56cm) |
| 7 | 22½in (57cm) |
| 8 | 23in (58cm) |
| 9 | 23½in (59cm) |
| 10 | 24in (60cm) |

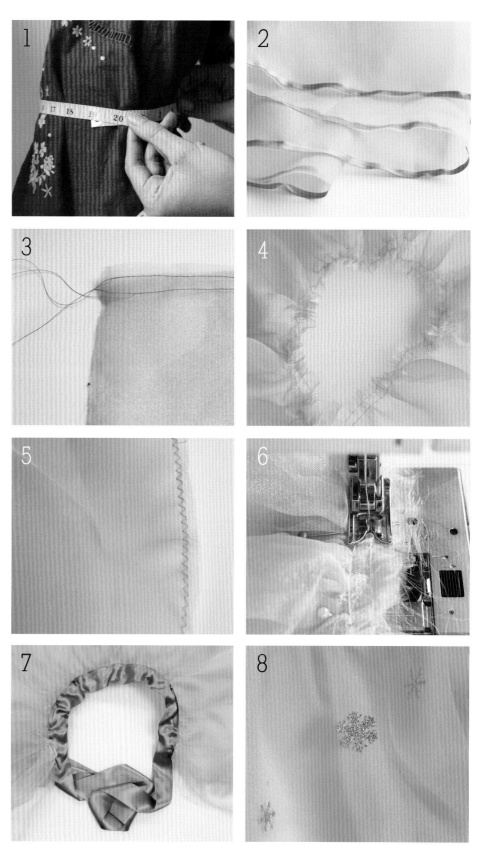

You could use contrasting threads in the needle and bobbin to help see which

## Step 1

Begin by measuring the waist of the child who will wear the skirt. For guidance, see the sizing chart opposite. From the blue organza, cut two pieces: one 2yd (1.8m) long x 14in (38cm) wide and another piece 2yd (1.8m) long and 13in (34cm) wide. From the white organza, cut a piece 2yd (1.8m) long x 12in (30cm) wide.

## Step 2

Pin coordinating ½in (1cm) wide ribbon along the bottom edge of each piece of fabric and sew in place with matching thread.

## Step 3

Set your sewing machine to the longest straight-stitch length (3 or 4). Pull the machine thread so there is 5in (12.5cm) of excess before you start to sew. Without back-stitching, sew two parallel lines of stitching along the top of each piece of fabric ½in (1cm) and 1in (2.5cm) from the top. When you get to the end, without back-stitching, cut the thread to leave a string of thread at least 5in (12.5cm) long.

## Step 4

Now to ruffle and gather the fabric. From one end, take the top threads of each line in one hand. Use your other hand to pull and gather the fabric towards you. Do a little, then repeat from the other end of the fabric. Continue until the fabric has reached the same length of the waist measurement that you took in Step 1. Tie the ends of the thread together. Adjust the ruffles so that they are even, then secure in place by sewing over the gathers, on top of your original stitches (set your machine back to a normal stitch length for this).

## Step 5

Sew a zigzag stitch along the short sides of each piece of fabric to stop it from fraying and neaten the edges. Trim off any excess material with sharp scissors.

## Step 6

Pin the three layers of skirt together at the waistband. Use a zigzag stitch to sew them together between the previous stitch lines.

## Step 7

Fold the wide piece of ribbon in half lengthways and iron it flat. Lay the ribbon out and place the waistband of the skirt in the center, sandwiched by the ribbon. Pin in place, then sew from one end of the ribbon to the other, along the open edge. Fold the ribbon ends over by ½in (1cm) and secure with a few hand stitches.

## Step 8

Glue the snowflake embellishments onto the first two layers of the skirt. As you do this, be careful to keep the layers apart to prevent the glue from sticking the skirt layers together.

threads to pull when gathering. They won't be visible when the ribbon is added.

# ROYAL HORSE

This beautiful steed is perfect for royal outings. She's very easy to make, with some simple sewing and a long piece of doweling or a broom handle. The horse has ribbon reins and a lovely woolen mane, which could even be plaited or styled with bows and accessories.

## You will need

- 1yd (1m) white corduroy fabric
- ¾oz (25g) ball of gray wool yarn
- 1½yd (1.25m) length of ¾in (2cm) wide purple ribbon
- Scraps of pink felt
- Black and white embroidery thread
- 2 x 1in (2.5cm) diameter black buttons
- Thick piece of doweling, at least 1in (2.5cm) in diameter
- 9oz (250g) bag of toy stuffing
- Duct tape
- Sewing machine
- Sewing needle and thread
- Templates for the horse's head and ears found on page 63

## Step 1

Photocopy the horse's head template from page 63 and cut it out. Fold the fabric in half and pin the template on top. If you are using corduroy, check the grain of the fabric before cutting so that it feels smooth when stroked from top to bottom. Cut around the template so that you have two head pieces for the horse.

## Step 2

To make the horse's mane, wrap yarn around a book measuring about 10in (25cm), 20 times to make a bundle, then cut the yarn and remove. Repeat this until you have enough bundles to fit tightly all the way down the neck of the horse (approximately 10 bundles).

## Step 3

Take one of the cut-out head pieces and pin the woolen bundles on the right side of the fabric, along the horse's neck. Start from roughly where the ears will go, down to 5in (12.5cm) from the bottom. The ends of the bundles should just overlap the edge of the fabric. Once all the bundles are pinned in place, carefully sew them onto the fabric with a ¼in (6mm) seam allowance.

## Step 4

Tuck the mane inside so that it is out of the way, then pin the two head pieces with right sides together. Sew them together with a ½in (1cm) allowance, starting at the bottom of the head and continuing all the way around to the other side, leaving the bottom open. Once sewn, snip notches around the curved edges then turn the right way out. Cut the loops of yarn to finish the mane.

## Step 5

Lightly fill the horse with toy stuffing. Mark on each side of the head where the eyes will be and sew on buttons. Stitch the eyelashes, nostrils, and a smile by hand with black embroidery thread, using the picture on page 32 for reference.

## Step 6

To make the ears, photocopy the template on page 63 and cut out four ear shapes from corduroy fabric. Cut two inner pieces from pink felt. Sew the felt onto the center of two corduroy pieces. Pin the ears with right sides together and sew with a ¼in (6mm) allowance, leaving the bottom open. Snip around the curved edges then turn the right way out. Press, folding the raw edges in at the bottom. Carefully sew the ears onto the top of the head by hand. Fill the head with more toy stuffing until it is sturdy.

## Step 7

For the reins, wrap ribbon around the nose, cut to size, and pin in place. Hand stitch at the bottom to secure. Tuck one end of the remaining ribbon into the nose piece by the mouth, and pin. Then take this length of ribbon under the eye, fold and pin at right angles, then over the forehead and repeat along the other side back to the nose. Pin in place and cut. The remaining ribbon will be the reins. Tuck each end under the folded corners and then carefully hand stitch all the pinned sections down.

## Step 8

Before inserting the pole into the horse, add a stopper to hold it in place and prevent it from ripping the fabric. Do this by wrapping a ball of scrap fabric around the top and securing this in place firmly with duct tape. Push the pole into the head. Add more stuffing so that the pole does not touch the fabric and sits solidly in the center of the head.

## Step 9

Fold up the bottom hem by 1in (2.5cm) and, using white embroidery thread with a knot tied in the end, hand sew a long running stitch along the hem. Pull the thread taught to gather the fabric together, then hand sew a few stitches across the hole, and knot to secure.

Sewing over the woolen bundles can be a little tricky, but don't worry if you miss a

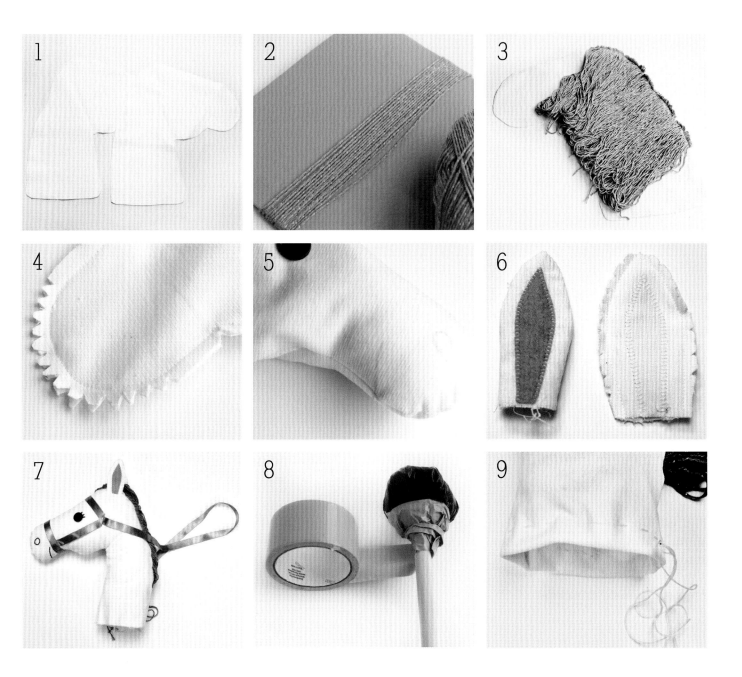

few strands when sewing. Hold the wool in place with your fingers as you sew.

# ROYAL THEATER

Made from an old picture frame, this royal theater is the perfect platform for the princess puppets on page 40. It's compact and freestanding, so it's ideal for impromptu tabletop shows. Your little ones can crouch behind the theater, open the curtains, and give all their royal guests an award-winning performance.

## You will need

- A large picture frame, about 8 x 10in (20 x 25cm)
- Gold and purple acrylic paint and paintbrush
- A piece of strong card (roughly the same size as the frame)
- A piece of red fabric (roughly the same size as the frame)
- 2 x eyelet hooks
- String
- PVA glue

- Strong glue
- 20in (50cm) gold ribbon
- Sewing needle and thread
- Scissors

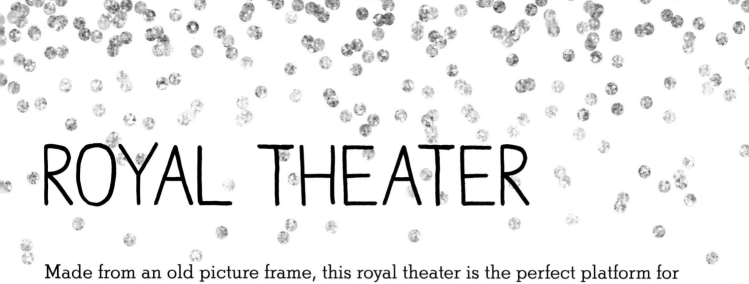

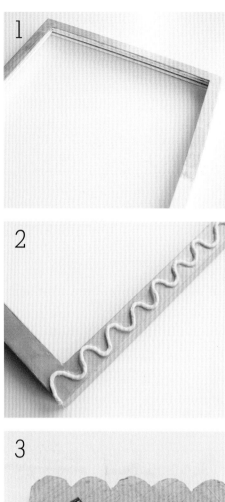

## Step 1

Remove and discard the backing and glass from the picture frame, then give it a good clean to ensure the paint will stick. Paint the front of the frame gold and the inside purple. You may need to paint several coats to cover it.

## Step 2

Pour a pool of PVA glue onto a plate. Cut a length of string, then dip and cover it in the glue. Arrange the string around the top and bottom of the frame to create a pattern (see finished photograph on page 37 for reference). Set the frame aside to dry, then paint over the string with gold paint.

## Step 3

Cut a strip of card the same width as the frame and about 2½in (6cm) tall. Create a scalloped shape along one of the long edges by repeatedly drawing around a small round coin, and cut out. Paint the strip of card with gold paint. When dry, glue the card along the top of the inside of the frame, with the scalloped edge pointing downward.

## Step 4

To make the frame stands, measure the inside height of the frame and cut two cardboard triangles to this height and 6in (15cm) deep. Paint both triangles with gold paint.

## Step 5

To make the curtains, cut the piece of red fabric in half vertically. Fold the tops over by 1in (2.5cm), pin down and hand sew in place.

## Step 6

Screw the eyelet hooks inside the frame at the top of each side and tie the string onto one of the hooks. Thread the curtains onto the string and tie the other end tightly on the other hook.

## Step 7

To make the curtain tiebacks, cut the gold ribbon in half. Glue to the inside of the frame in the center. Use strong glue to attach the stands to each side, over the gold ribbon.

Make sure you soak the string in glue so that it can easily be molded into place.

**5**

**6**

**7**

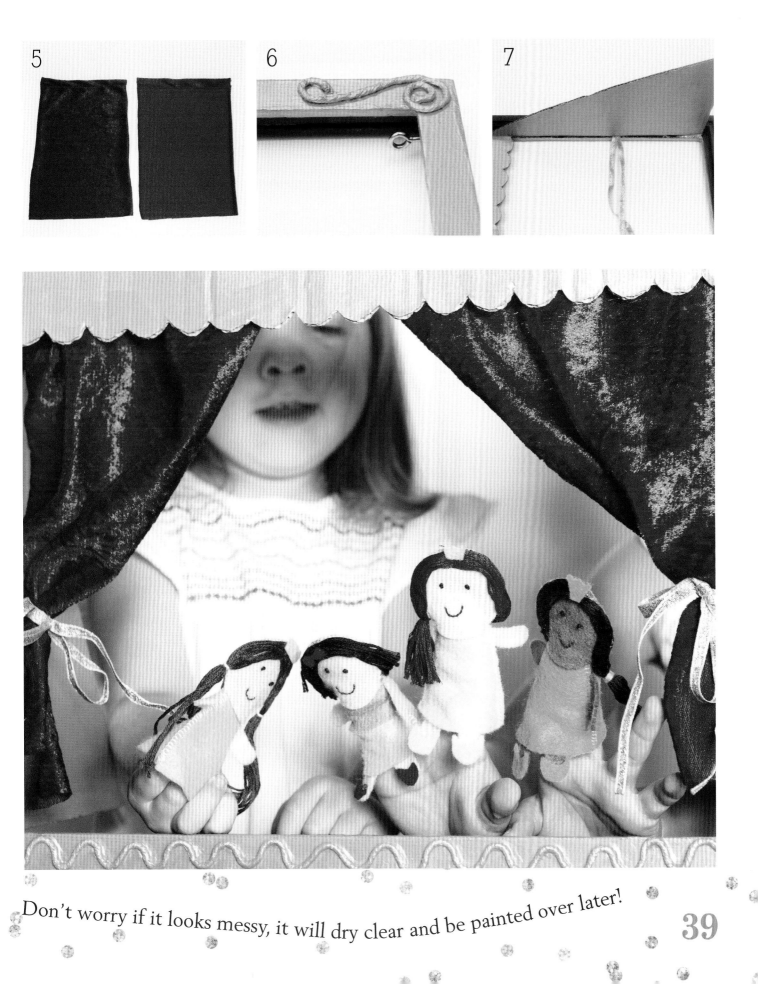

Don't worry if it looks messy, it will dry clear and be painted over later!

# PRINCESS FINGER PUPPETS

Act out your favorite fairytales with these mini majesties. A little cutting, sewing, and gluing will give you a palace full of little characters in no time—and the best thing is they're always on hand! The puppets are made from felt so they can easily be glued and stitched by hand, or on a sewing machine.

## You will need

**To make one puppet:**

- Scraps of felt in pink, yellow, and brown (more colors for other puppets)
- 50in (127cm) brown embroidery thread for hair, and a small amount of black and red thread for the face (more colors for other puppets)

- PVA glue
- Sewing needle
- Scissors
- Templates for the head/hair, body, arm/leg, crown, shoe, and foot found on page 63

## Step 1

Photocopy the templates on page 63 and cut them out. From the pink felt, cut two arms and two legs. Then cut one circle from the pink and one from the brown felt. From the yellow felt, cut two body pieces, two little shoes to cover the feet, and a small crown. Glue the pink circle onto the front body piece for the face, the brown circle onto the back body piece for the back of the hair, the shoes onto the legs, and the legs on the reverse of the front body piece.

## Step 2

To make the hair, cut about ten 5in (12.5cm) lengths of brown embroidery thread. You can do this by looping the thread around your hands. Pin the thread to the top of the face and either glue or sew a few stitches to secure it in place at the top of the head. Then cut the ends of the loops to create strands of hair.

## Step 3

Mark in pencil two dots for eyes and a smile onto the face. Then knot a piece of black embroidery thread and sew on eyes using French knots. To do this, pull the thread from the back of the fabric, then wrap it around the needle three times, holding the thread so it is tightly wrapped around the needle. Push the needle back through the felt and pull tight.

## Step 4

Knot a piece of red embroidery thread and sew on a mouth using backstitch.

## Step 5

To sew the doll together, sandwich the arms between the front and back body pieces and hand sew using blanket stitch, starting at one corner of the dress and working up and around the head down to the other corner. Move the hair out of the way as you go. Leave a gap along the bottom of the dress, big enough for a finger.

## Step 6

Dab some glue around the side of the puppet's face and glue the hair down a little. Once dry, you can give the princess a royal hairstyle. You could plait the hair, give her pigtails, or leave it loose. Secure the hairstyle by tying the same color thread around it. The final touch is to glue the tiny felt crown to the top of the hair.

Make the Royal Theater on page 36 to create a handy freestanding stage

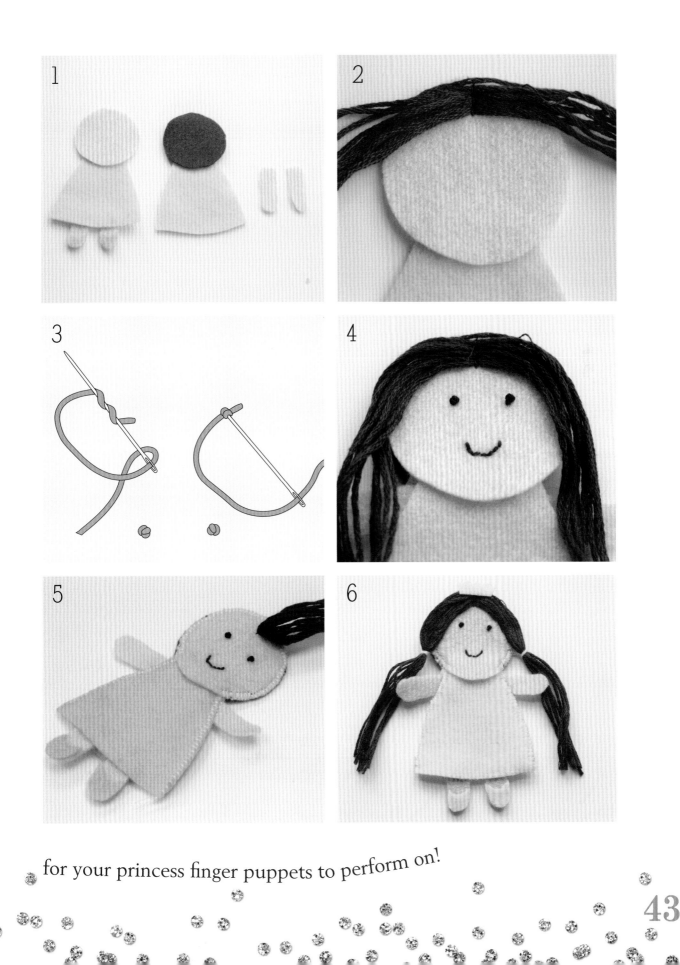

for your princess finger puppets to perform on!

# A SNOW QUEEN SNOW GLOBE

Create a sparkly winter scene with just a few materials and a little bit of time. This project uses polymer clay, which is ideal because it is colorful, easy to work, and waterproof. You can use pretty much any jar, as long as the glass is clear and smooth. Bear in mind that you will need to make the clay model to fit the jar, so keep the lid handy as a size guide when you are making it.

## You will need

♡ 1½in (4cm) cube white polymer clay

♡ 2in (5cm) cube blue polymer clay

♡ 1in (2.5cm) cube pale pink polymer clay

♡ Pea-sized piece gray polymer clay (optional)

♡ Pencil

♡ Permanent fine-line markers in blue, black, and red

♡ Parchment paper

♡ Glitter

♡ Sequins

♡ Glass jar (with labels removed)

♡ PVA glue

♡ Strong (waterproof) glue

♡ Rolling pin

♡ Knife

♡ Plate

## Step 1

Get a clean plate to work on, and wash your hands to prevent the clay from getting dirty—it very easily picks up dust and fluff. To make the cape you will need a piece of pale blue clay, which you can easily make by mixing the blue and white together. Work the clay between your fingers so that it is warm and malleable. Roll into a 1in (2.5cm) ball and place between two pieces of parchment paper. Roll until the clay is ¼in (6mm) thick and gently peel it away from the paper. Cut the clay into a cape shape, which should be narrower at the top with a slightly rounded base, as shown.

## Step 2

To make the body, take a thumb-sized piece of blue clay and roll it between your fingers to create a cone shape. Roll a piece of pale pink clay to create a sausage shape about ¼in (6mm) thick and 2½in (6cm) long, then cut this in half to create two arms. Roll another piece of pale pink clay to create a 1in (2.5cm) ball for the head.

## Step 3

Attach the arms in position on the body and press in place.

## Step 4

Place the cape onto the body around the arms and smooth down. Roll the top of the body slightly between your fingers to combine the clay.

## Step 5

To make the hair, roll out a ¾in (2cm) cube of white clay into a ball, then roll out flat between parchment paper so that you have an oval-shaped piece of clay that is about 2½in (6cm) wide and ¹⁄₁₆in (2mm) thick. Cut out a 1in (2.5cm) triangle shape from one of the longer sides to create a parting to frame the face. Roll another long sausage of white clay and cut it into three pieces (each about 2½in/6cm long). Place these alongside each other, pinch together at the top, then plait all the way down. Pinch and roll slightly at the bottom again to secure.

## Step 6

Gently smooth the white clay onto the head and wrap it around so that it resembles hair around a face. Pinch the clay at the back of the head and cut off the excess with a knife.

## Step 7

Attach the plait to the back of the head over the cut section. Use your fingers and the front of your fingernails to smooth the hair.

## Step 8

Attach the head to the body and press down to secure. Take a tiny piece of gray clay and roll to form two small sausages. Attach in an 'X' shape to form a fastener for the cape. Arrange the hair around the body and press in place. Bake the clay on a sheet of parchment paper on a low heat, following the manufacturer's instructions.

## Step 9

When the doll has cooled, use a pencil to mark the features on her little face, then draw them in with permanent fine-line markers.

## Step 10

Paint the outside of the lid of the jar with PVA glue. Place it on a piece of card and sprinkle glitter liberally all over the top. Tip away the excess and leave the jar to dry.

## Step 11

Use strong waterproof glue to attach the doll onto the inside of the jar lid. Check that she is properly lined up in the center and make sure the jar can fit back on top before the glue sets. Sprinkle some glitter and sequins into the jar.

## Step 12

Gently fill the jar to the top with water and screw the lid back on. Some water will spill out of the top—this is okay because it means there will be no air bubbles inside. If you want to make it extra secure, paste some strong waterproof glue around the edge of the lid before you put it back on the jar. Shake the snow globe and place it in a sunny spot for extra sparkles!

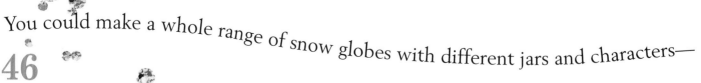

You could make a whole range of snow globes with different jars and characters—

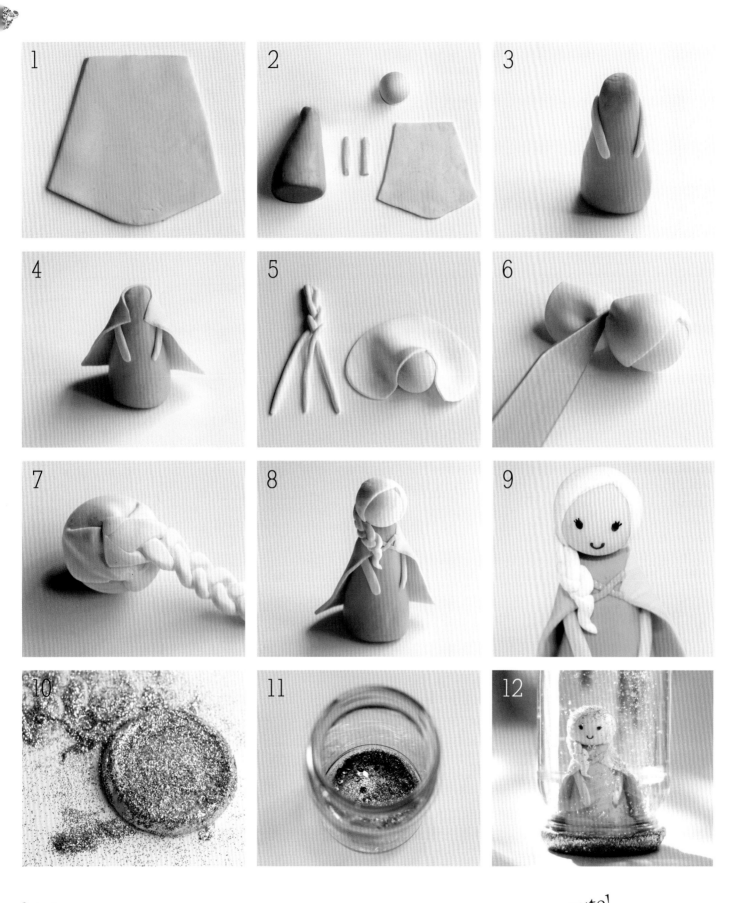

a mini snowman globe made from a baby-food jar would be very cute!

# RAPUNZEL HAIR BRAID

This braid is very simple to make, all you need is a ball of yarn! This one is long and golden, just like Rapunzel's, but you could make it in a variety of colors, styles, and lengths for different princesses. Try ruby red for a mermaid or white with snowflakes for a snow queen. Involve your little one in the making process by teaching them how to do a braid.

## You will need

♡ 1¾oz (50g) ball of yellow wool yarn

♡ Scraps of pastel-colored felt

♡ 7 x colored buttons

♡ 10in (25cm) length of ½in (1cm) wide ribbon

♡ Strong glue

♡ Scissors

♡ Template for flower on page 63

To make it easier to plait the length of hair, hang one end of the braid

## Step 1

Pull a strand of yarn to a length of around 47in (120cm). Fold it back on itself to create a series of loops that are the same length. Keep going until there are about 25 loops, then cut the yarn. You may want to ask someone to hold one end for you while you do this, or wrap the loops around a chair.

## Step 2

Take another 47in (120cm) long strand of yarn and tie in the center of the hair to secure. The excess strands will hang to form part of the bunch. Cut through the loops at each end.

## Step 3

Measure the circumference of your child's head and divide this number by two. Working from the tied center of the hair outward, make two plaits, one on each side of the center. Each of these plaits needs to measure the length of half the circumference of your child's head. Take another 1yd (1m) length of yarn and tie the two plaits together (again, the excess will form part of the bunch). You should now have a braided loop that fits on your child's head—if it is too big or too small, adjust where you tie it.

## Step 4

Plait the remaining length of hair as one. Tie at the end with another short strand of wool. Trim the ends to ensure they are all the same length.

## Step 5

To make the flowers, cut small flower shapes from felt using the template found on page 63. Place one at an angle on top of another and glue them together, then glue a matching button on top.

## Step 6

Glue the flowers along the hair and tie a piece of ribbon in a bow around the end of the plait.

onto something while you work, like a door handle or the back of a chair.

# SPARKLY ICE QUEEN GLOVES

Whether your princess is waving at crowds, or having to conceal magical powers, she'll want a pair of jeweled gloves. As the perfect finishing touch to a royal outfit, these couldn't be easier to make. Shiny satin-effect gloves like the ones used here are readily available and are perfect for precious princess hands.

## You will need

- ♡ A pair of satin-effect dressing-up gloves
- ♡ Plastic gems in a variety of sizes
- ♡ 13in (32cm) length of silver rickrack trim
- ♡ Strong glue
- ♡ Gray or silver thread
- ♡ A few sheets of rolled-up paper
- ♡ Tweezers
- ♡ Pencil

## Step 1

Begin by cutting the rickrack trim in half and pinning it around the bottom edge of the gloves.

## Step 2

Hand stitch the rickrack in place using gray or silver thread.

## Step 3

Place gems onto one of the gloves and play around with them until you are happy with the design, then using a pen or pencil, mark out where you placed each one with small dots.

## Step 4

Place rolled-up paper inside the gloves to prevent them from sticking together. Use strong glue to carefully place the gems onto the gloves—use tweezers if this is a little fiddly.

When applying glue to the gems, use a tiny amount as too much will spread onto the

## OTHER IDEAS

These gloves are super simple, but why stop there? You could add sparkle to other items too. Why not glam up a pair of canvas pumps, or a matching satin bag, for example?

gloves and mark them. Dot the gems on gently so the glue doesn't leak out at the sides.

# THE ULTIMATE PRINCESS PARTY

Every princess deserves a special party to celebrate in style. Add a bit of magic and sparkle to create an event that will receive a royal seal of approval. With nibbles and games, these party ideas will keep a room full of VIP guests entertained.

## PARTY NIBBLES

### Castle cake
See page 58 for details on how to make a simple castle cake.

### Kiss-the-frog cookies
Use a frog-shaped cutter to make simple cookies. Decorate with vivid green icing and use black writing icing to add eyes and a mouth.

### Mini tiara pizzas
Make your own mini tiara-shaped pizzas by cutting crown shapes into bases, then adding the toppings. Sweetcorn, olives, and pineapple make great pizza jewels. Little princesses could even decorate their own tiaras as a fun party activity.

### Crispy rice-cereal wands
Make a batch of crispy rice-cereal bites using a star-shaped cookie cutter. Attach a lollipop stick before they have set, and drizzle the cakes with white chocolate, or sprinkle on sugar strands and edible glitter.

## PARTY GAMES

### Dress-up box
Having a basket of necklaces, tiaras, gloves, and rings will be a big party hit. This would also be a great prop box for a mini photo booth. All you need is a large, empty picture frame for princesses to pose behind. For older princesses, create a dressing-up relay race.

### Jewel hunt
Hide precious gems around the party area and ask the little princesses to hunt them out. Older children could follow clues, or even a treasure map, to find their gems.

### Crown toss
Make simple crowns from card—the kids could decorate their own. Place a hula hoop on the grass (or a stick in the grass for older kids) and ask the children to try and throw the crowns as close to the goal as possible.

### Wand decorating
Make a batch of our salt-dough wands (see page 16) on lollipop sticks in advance of the party. The princesses can decorate them with paint, stickers, ribbons, and glitter. Make sure you have enough aprons to cover up best dresses.

### Crown piñata
Construct a large crown out of cardboard boxes and cover with layers of yellow crepe paper. Fill with royal goodies and see if the children can bash them out.

### Pin the glass slipper onto the princess
Draw a bare-footed princess on a large piece of card. Wearing a blindfold, the princesses take it in turns to try and place a cardboard slipper onto the picture in the correct position.

# PRINCESS CASTLE CAKE

Every birthday princess needs a royal cake to celebrate in style. And this one is very easy—suitable even for the complete beginner. You can choose any flavor of sponge cake and any color for the icing to suit your party theme.

## You will need

- ♡ 2 sponge cakes, 9 x 9in (23 x 23cm) (either store-bought or made to your own recipe)
- ♡ 1lb 12oz (800g) vanilla buttercream frosting (either store-bought or made to your own recipe)
- ♡ 2lb 3¼oz (1kg) pink, ready-to-use fondant
- ♡ 5¼oz (150g) apricot jam
- ♡ 1lb 2oz (500g) white, ready-to-use fondant
- ♡ 5 x ice-cream cones
- ♡ Hundreds and thousands sprinkles
- ♡ 3 pink sugar wafers

- ♡ 5½oz (160g) bag gumdrops
- ♡ 2¾oz (80g) white chocolate buttons or candy melts
- ♡ Confectioners' sugar, for dusting
- ♡ 2½in (6cm) diameter cookie cutter
- ♡ Sharp knife
- ♡ Wax paper
- ♡ Plastic wrap
- ♡ Rolling pin
- ♡ 5 x wooden skewers (cut in half)

## Step 1

If you are making your sponges, let them cool completely before you start working. Use a 2in (6cm) diameter cookie cutter to cut ten circles from around the edges of one of the cakes. Cut the remainder of the cake to form a square that should measure about 5in (12.5cm).

## Step 2

Place wax paper or plastic wrap onto a counter and roll out 200g (7oz) of pink fondant. Sprinkle a small amount of confectioners' sugar on top of the fondant so it doesn't stick to the rolling pin. It should be 2in (5cm) bigger than your small square cake, with a thickness of approximately $\frac{1}{16}$in (2mm). Spread a thin layer of slightly melted apricot jam over the top and sides of the small cake.

## Step 3

Lift up the rolled-out fondant while it is still on the wax paper and place it on top of the cake. Pinch the edges of the fondant to emphasize the corners and smooth out any lumps with your fingers. Use a sharp knife to cut off the excess fondant from the bottom. Use the rest of the pink fondant to repeat steps 2 and 3 for the larger cake.

## Step 4

Spread a layer of frosting onto the bottom of the smaller square cake and place it on top of the larger cake.

## Step 5

To make the towers, pile up two sponge circles with a layer of frosting in between. Insert half a wooden skewer into the rounds to keep them together. Cover each in a thin layer of frosting and place in the fridge for about an hour to harden.

## Step 6

Roll out 18oz (500g) of white fondant between two lengths of plastic wrap to a thickness of approximately $\frac{1}{16}$in (2mm). Cut five fondant strips measuring 3 x 8in (7.5 x 20cm). Place each tower on top of the strips and push the skewer through the bottom of each tower to make it easier to handle. Roll the fondant around the tower and smooth the ends together with your fingers.

## Step 7

Place a tower onto each corner of the cake and one in the center. Push skewers into the cake to hold the towers in place, but make sure the ends stick out a little so that you can remove them before serving.

## Step 8

To make the turrets, spread a thin layer of frosting over the outside of the ice-cream cones. Tip a generous amount of hundreds and thousands onto a plate and roll the cones until they are completely covered.

## Step 9

Spread a layer of frosting on top of each tower and place the ice-cream cone turrets on top.

You could add personalized paper flags to the top of the cake, or even some

## Step 10

Make a paste by mixing a little water and icing sugar to form a glue-like consistency. Stick gumdrops around the bottom of the turrets and chocolate buttons around the walls. Cut small windows (about ½ x 1in/1 x 2.5cm) from pink sugar wafers and attach these to the towers. Roll a thin tube (approximately ¼in/6mm) of pink fondant and wrap around the bottom of the cone turrets.

## Step 11

To make the doors, slice a sugar wafer diagonally though the middle and attach them to the larger cake in the center, then add a gumdrop door handle with paste.

marzipan princesses to guard the gates.

# TEMPLATES

Templates that are shown at actual size can be traced and cut out, or photocopied. For templates that have been reduced in size, enlarge them on a photocopier to the percentage stated. Align each template as near to the top left-hand corner of the photocopier glass as possible. You may need to repeat this a few times to find the best position.

Heart Handbag and Charm (see page 4)

Shrink Plastic Jewels (see page 8)

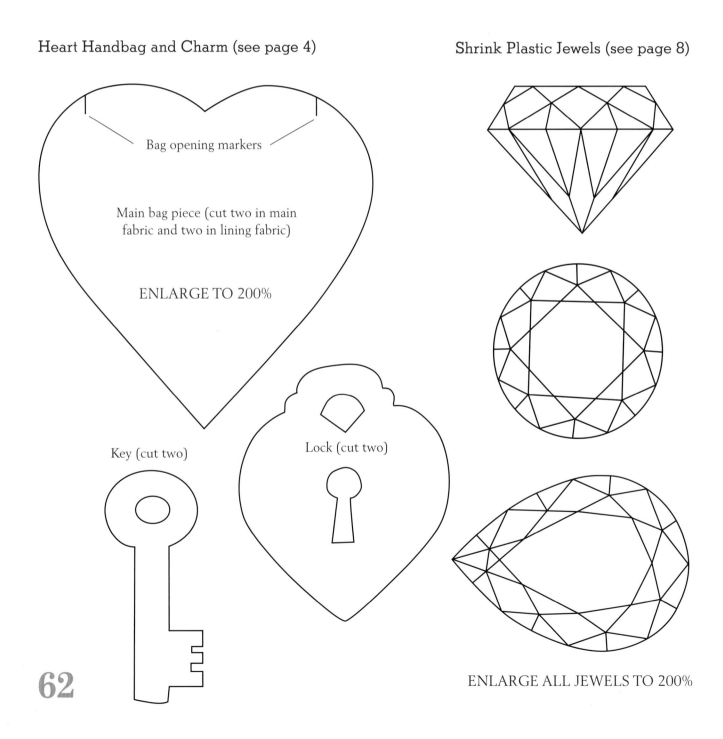

Bag opening markers

Main bag piece (cut two in main fabric and two in lining fabric)

ENLARGE TO 200%

Key (cut two)

Lock (cut two)

ENLARGE ALL JEWELS TO 200%

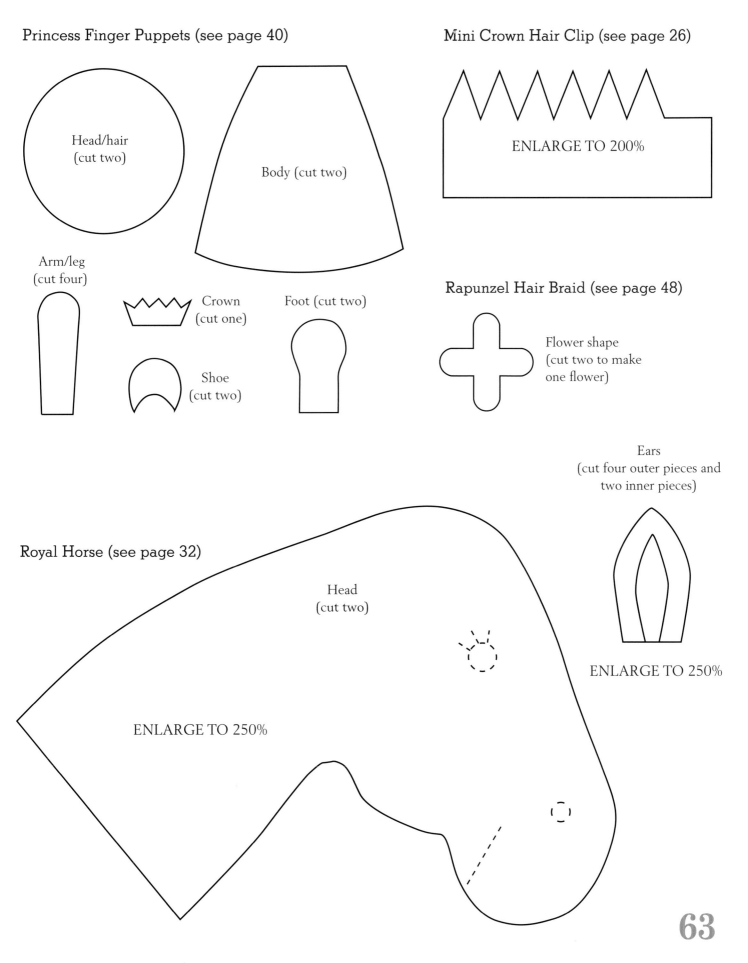

Princess Finger Puppets (see page 40)

Head/hair
(cut two)

Body (cut two)

Mini Crown Hair Clip (see page 26)

ENLARGE TO 200%

Arm/leg
(cut four)

Crown
(cut one)

Foot (cut two)

Shoe
(cut two)

Rapunzel Hair Braid (see page 48)

Flower shape
(cut two to make
one flower)

Ears
(cut four outer pieces and
two inner pieces)

Royal Horse (see page 32)

Head
(cut two)

ENLARGE TO 250%

ENLARGE TO 250%

Laura Minter and Tia Williams are two creative mums who started *Little Button Diaries*, their award-winning crafting and baking blog, to show that having children doesn't mean you have to stop doing the things you love. They also write craft tutorials for craft superstore *Hobbycraft*, and major retailers *Paperchase* and *Laura Ashley*. Between them, they have four children who they love to make things for (and with!).
www.littlebuttondiaries.com

To place an order, or to request a catalog, contact:

GMC Publications Ltd, Castle Place, 166 High Street, Lewes, East Sussex, BN7 1XU, United Kingdom

Tel: +44 (0)1273 488005
www.gmcbooks.com